CONCERTO No.1 IN G, K.313

Edited by Trevor Wye
Piano arrangement by Robert Scott

W. A. MOZART

1

FLUTE

(or)*

* See Preface

© Copyright 1983 Novello & Company Limited

Order No: NOV120577

*See Preface   † In some modern editions the G sharp appears three notes earlier.

* An F♯ appears here in some editions. It makes musical sense but until an autograph is found, doubts will remain.

4

FLUTE

† In some modern editions the C sharp appears three notes earlier.

181

184

(p)

188

(p)

192

(cresc.)

199

(mf)

203

206

(cresc.)

209

(f)

(See Preface)

(f)

2

32

35 *(dim.)*

38 *(p)*

41 *(cresc.)* *(p)*

45

47

50

52 *(f)* (See Preface)

57 *(p)*

61 6 *(fp)*

3

Rondo. Tempo di Menuetto

CADENZAS

To write your own cadenza based on the concerto, first look at the useful thematic material:

1st Movement

2nd Movement

3rd Movement

When you have looked at the possibilities, find a short phrase which links the pause to the final trill.
For example:-

You don't have to start on the written note at the beginning of a cadenza, nor do you have to trill the written note. A trill on F sharp would do just as well. When you gain experience, you may even omit the trill altogether, and re-enter the movement without the usual trilled preparation, thus surprising the audience.

Without attempting to modulate, try inserting another piece of material which, in turn, leads to the cadence:

This is by no means a cadenza yet, but it is a start. Now extend your cadenza as necessary, using themes from the concerto or your own material.

Keep the cadenza simple to begin with. You should only modulate when you are more experienced in writing them, and even then, no more than twice in one cadenza.

Finally, try to play your cadenza spontaneously as if you are making it up as you go along.

If you are playing with a piano, the pianist might put in the dominant seventh chord half-way through the final trill in order to resolve the previous six-four chord, and so maintain the forward movement. The chord is indicated in this edition.

Be patient; don't expect an immediate and brilliant result; only Mozart could do that.

Below can be found some simple sample cadenzas for your use.

Trevor Wye 1991

1st Movement

2nd Movement

3rd Movement

MUSIC FOR FLUTE

TUTORS

WYE, Trevor
A BEGINNER'S BOOK FOR THE FLUTE
Part 1 (Cassette also available)
Part 2

A PRACTICE BOOK FOR THE FLUTE:
VOLUME 1 Tone (Cassette also available)
VOLUME 2 Technique
VOLUME 3 Articulation
VOLUME 4 Intonation and vibrato
VOLUME 5 Breathing and scales
VOLUME 6 Advanced Practice
PROPER FLUTE PLAYING

SOLO

ALBUM
ed Trevor Wye
MUSIC FOR SOLO FLUTE
This attractive collection draws together under
one cover 11 major works representing the
fundamental solo flute repertoire, edited in a
clear and practical form.

trans Gordon Saunders
EIGHT TRADITIONAL JAPANESE PIECES
Gordon Saunders has selected and transcribed
these pieces for tenor recorder solo or flute from
the traditional folk music of Japan.

FLUTE AND PIANO

ALBUMS
arr Barrie Carson Turner
CHRISTMAS FUN BOOK
CLASSICAL POPS FUN BOOK
ITALIAN OPERA FUN BOOK
MOZART FUN BOOK
POP CANTATA FUN BOOK
POPULAR CLASSICS FUN BOOK
RAGTIME FUN BOOK
TV THEME FUN BOOK

arr Trevor Wye
A VERY EASY BAROQUE ALBUM, Vols. 1 & 2
A VERY EASY CLASSICAL ALBUM
A VERY EASY ROMANTIC ALBUM
A VERY EASY 20TH CENTURY ALBUM
A FIRST LATIN-AMERICAN FLUTE ALBUM
A SECOND LATIN-AMERICAN FLUTE ALBUM

BENNETT, Richard Rodney
SUMMER MUSIC

COUPERIN, François
arr Trevor Wye
A COUPERIN ALBUM

ELGAR, Edward
arr Trevor Wye
AN ELGAR FLUTE ALBUM

FAURE, Gabriel
arr Trevor Wye
A FAURE ALBUM

FRASER, Shena
SONATINA

GALWAY, James
THE MAGIC FLUTE OF JAMES GALWAY
SHOWPIECES

HARRIS, Paul
CLOWNS

HURD, Michael
SONATINA

McCABE, John
PORTRAITS

RAMEAU, Jean Philippe
arr Trevor Wye
A RAMEAU ALBUM

RAVEL, Maurice
arr Trevor Wye
A RAVEL ALBUM

REEMAN, John
SIX FOR ONE

SATIE, Erik
arr Trevor Wye
A SATIE FLUTE ALBUM

SCHUBERT, Franz
arr Trevor Wye
THEME AND VARIATIONS D.935 No.3

SCHUMANN, Robert
arr Trevor Wye
A SCHUMANN ALBUM

SCHURMANN, Gerard
SONATINA

VIVALDI, Antonio
arr Trevor Wye
A VIVALDI ALBUM

NOVELLO